Confident & Competent

A CHALLENGE FOR THE LAY CHURCH

Confident & Competent

A CHALLENGE FOR THE LAY CHURCH

William L. Droel & Gregory F. Augustine Pierce

Foreword by Msgr. George G. Higgins

AVE MARIA PRESS   Notre Dame, IN 46556

To Mary Ann and Kathy
Our best friend's best friend.

CONTENTS

Foreword

A generation of lay leadership may have been lost because of the Catholic church's preoccupation with internal affairs and a devaluation of the laity's social responsibility.

That was the gist of "A Chicago Declaration of Christian Concern," a statement issued on the third Sunday of Advent, 1977, by a group of Chicago area Catholics and directed to the church in the United States.

The statement pointed to three post-Vatican II developments among American Catholics that in their opinion had led to the devaluation of the laity's social responsibility: The first was the movement to involve laypersons in the church's official ministries with decreasing emphasis on the secular mission of the laity; the second, the tendency of some members of the clergy to pre-empt the layperson's responsibility for social reform; the third, a trend of diminishing interest in Christian social thought as the mediating ground between the gospel and specific political and economic issues.

The drafters of the statement said they were waiting "impatiently for a new prophecy, a new word that can once again stir the laity to see the grandeur of the Christian vision for man in society and move priests to galvanize laypersons in their secular-religious role." They pointed out that in the last analysis, "the Church speaks to and acts upon the world through her laity" and that "without a dynamic laity conscious of its ministry to the world, the Church in effect does not speak or act. . . . It would be one of the great ironies of history if the era of Vatican II which opened windows of the Church to the world were to close with the Church turned in upon herself."

The slim but meaty book which I am privileged to introduce in this Foreword is, in summary, an extended commentary and elaboration on the main themes of the Chicago Declaration. The authors—both Easterners who have faced the culture shock of becoming naturalized citizens of Chicago—did not sign the Declaration and were not involved in the consultative process that led to its publication in 1977. In the main, however, they agree with its basic thrust and, on the basis of their own experience and in the light of post-1977 developments in the church, have attempted here to flesh the statement out, so to speak, and to bring it up-to-date. In my opinion, they have done so admirably well. Moreover, in view of the fact that the 1987 Synod of Bishops deals with the role of the laity, their timing is providentially perfect. Their book is required reading for all of the synodal delegates.

When the Chicago Declaration was issued in

1977, I said in print that, in my opinion, its drafters had performed a useful service to the U.S. Catholic community. I added, however, that while I agreed with the statement, at least in its main lines, I did not mean to suggest—nor did its sponsors pretend—that it was the last word on the subject under discussion. The authors of the present volume gracefully make the same disclaimer. They state right up front in their Preface that while they have some definite opinions about the Catholic church in the United States, "we are well aware that others will disagree with some or all of our observations, and we trust that this will not be the last word on this subject, either from us or from others reflecting on the role of the laity."

This emboldens me to say that while I do not "disagree" with their major conclusions and recommendations, I would tentatively be inclined to nuance or modify some of them. Two examples will suffice. In Chapter IV the authors state flatly and without qualification that "the teaching of the 'preferential option for the poor' discourages those laypeople who are following a middle-class road to sanctity." In support of this statement, they argue that decision-making in people's normal lives regularly involves conflicting values and mixed motives. Yet "the church in preparation and reflection" often ignores this reality. There is, I suppose, a germ of truth to this argument, but, in my judgment, it is stated much too sweepingly and simplistically. Moreover, I suspect that many members of the middle class may find it rather patronizing.

Similarly, the authors' treatment of self-interest raises almost as many questions as it answers. I think I know what the authors are driving at but, again, I have the uneasy feeling that they have stated their argument too simplistically. In addition, I am afraid that, in doing so, they may have unwittingly left the impression that they have opted ideologically for the so-called neo-conservative point of view (as symbolized, for example, by the writings of Charles Murray) in the current political debate about the pros and cons of the welfare system in the United States. Surely that's a legitimate point of view, but it cries out for much more supporting evidence than the authors have provided here.

These are minor points. I have raised them only to keep the dialogue going or, if you will, to keep the authors on their toes. In general, I think they have served us all very well by re-emphasizing and elaborating upon the main themes of the Chicago Declaration. Respectfully, however, I would suggest, in conclusion, that while we badly need and can profit greatly from books of this kind, what we need even more 20 years after Vatican II, is the living example of lay-initiated programs based on the principles of the Declaration which the authors have fleshed out so convincingly. The laity have the right to expect the "official" church to respect these principles in theory and to help the laity implement them in practice. In short, the authors are correct when they say that "there is a tremendous need for programs to support the laity in their vocation to job, family and neighborhood." Experience suggests, however, that lay initiative in developing programs of this type is indispensable. To spend too much time and energy theorizing about the role of the laity or lamenting the failure of official church leaders to take the lead in this area is, in my opinion, to sell the laity short and, even worse, to encourage a new form of post-Vatican II clericalism. I am not suggesting that the authors of the present book or the drafters of the Chicago Declaration have unwittingly fallen into this trap. To the contrary, they have played an indispensable role in clarifying the role of the laity in the life of the church in the United States. It would be a mistake, however, to think that books and statements alone will bring about the changes that they are rightly calling for. In short, the time has come for a new burst of lay-initiated action of the type (if I may say so chauvinistically) that made Chicago famous in the '40s and '50s. It is my hope and expectation that this excellent book will serve as a timely catalyst in this regard. I recommend the book enthusiastically.

Monsignor George G. Higgins
Washington, D.C.
May 19, 1986

Preface

In many ways *Confident and Competent* is a conservative book. This surprises us, because we have always thought of ourselves as liberals, if not radicals. It is curious, too, because *Confident and Competent* advocates many basic changes.

This is why *Confident and Competent* is conservative:

1. We believe in the institutional church. Many in our generation do not. At times we, too, wonder if perhaps the institutional church has done more harm than good. The church's insensitivity to women is only a current example of its frailty. Our life experience, however, has confirmed the importance of institutions in general and the institutional church specifically. We are both involved in the institutional church and have worked for many years in church-based community organizations.

2. We believe in the hierarchical nature of the church. Not that we think that the bishops and priests should make all the decisions, while those in the pews "pray, pay and obey." But we do see the benefit of a hierarchy of functions. When each level of the hierarchy attends to its competency, reform can be implemented efficiently, while tradition can be preserved.

3. We have an unapologetic love affair with the American democratic experiment and its achievements. We believe that American political philosophy contains a liberating dynamic, new to human history. Our grandparents and great-grandparents fled poverty in Europe. Their children, our parents, enjoy liberty in the United States and have been able to become generous members of the human family. We believe that there are defects in the American system, and that certain races and classes have borne the burden for those defects. Yet we know that American institutions can be reformed. Our love for our country runs so deep that we have endured the boredom of thousands of community meetings and the anxiety of many direct actions to create peaceful social change.

4. We respect the method and accomplishments of gradual, institutional reform undertaken in the name of Catholic social teaching. While we truly admire the Dorothy Days, the Berrigans, the James Douglasses, we are critical when their prophetic mode is advanced as the only possible, or even the best, method of change. For ourselves, we have chosen a path of activism that relies on neither guilt, self-denial nor pure altruism. We have chosen to worry about ourselves, our families and friends, our jobs, our neighborhoods, our country in relation to the needs of others. We operate in our self-interest.

Confident and Competent has some definite opinions about the Catholic church in the United States. We are well aware that others will disagree with some or all of our observations, and we trust that this will not be the last word on this subject, either from us or from others reflecting on the role of the laity.

We must acknowledge the debt our thinking on this issue owes to the strong lay movement in Chicago over the past 50 years. We are particularly indebted to the 47 signers of the 1977 *Chicago Declaration Of Christian Concern*. Though the phrasing of that document needs updating, it serves as a seminal reflection on the missed opportunities in the American Catholic church since Vatican II. The National Center for the Laity, based in Chicago and with which we are associated, is dedicated to continuous exploration of the vocation of laypeople in and to the world.

Our thanks to Russell Barta, Charles DiSalvo and Oliver Williams for their comments on early drafts of this book, and to George Higgins for his erudite foreword. Finally, our special thanks to Frank Cunningham, the Managing Editor at Ave Maria Press, who—while not agreeing with everything we have to say—made this book possible.

William L. Droel
Gregory F. Augustine Pierce

Introduction:

Confident and Competent

There are different kinds of spiritual gifts, but the same Spirit gives them. There are different ways of serving, but the same Lord is served. There are different abilities to perform service, but the same God gives ability to everyone for their particular service.

—*1 Corinthians 12:4-6*

When the American participants in the Second Vatican Council returned home, they initiated great changes in the Catholic church. Liturgies, prayed in the vernacular, became celebrations of community. The ornamental family bible was replaced with the living word of God. Clericalism began to disappear as the laity began to assume important responsibilities for church administration and ministry.

In their new roles as parish council members, permanent deacons, lectors, directors of religious education, and diocesan and parish administrators, Catholic laity have democratized the church in a new way. The current emphasis on "paraclerical" lay ministries, however, contains the danger that the church—hierarchy, clergy, religious and laity alike—will lose sight of the lay vocation to be church in and to the modern world.

The church in the modern world, as mandated by Vatican II, the church that evangelizes culture, politics and the economy has to be a lay-centered church. The teaching of Vatican II depends on the laity taking a role in sustaining and improving the world:

> The laity, by their very vocation, seek the kingdom of God by engaging in temporal affairs and by ordering them to the plan of God. They live in the world, that is, in each and in all of the secular professions and occupations. . . .
> . . . They can work for the sanctification of the world from within, in the manner of leaven.[1]

The Catholic church is at one of those critical moments when it must remember that it is a means, not an end. Current crises of membership, finances and staffing can easily lead to an overemphasis on internal church matters to the neglect of a serious and effective concern for the laity's vocation in and to the world.

In all institutions those who are supposed to be served (customers, stockholders, union members, students, citizens, consumers) must maintain a vested interest in the conduct of their institutions. In the church, therefore, the laity must be involved with its internal functioning. Many of the changes since Vatican II to increase lay participation in the operation and governance of the church are right and just.

Those who are involved in the management of the church, however—be they ordained or not—can never forget that the purpose of that involvement is to serve the people of God who minister in the world. Any institution that spends too much time, energy and money on its internal problems tends to neglect its external mission.

If the mission of the church to the world is neglected, laypeople will soon begin to think that their daily struggles are not important and that only work within church structures is salvific. As Bishop Paul Cordes, Vice President of the Vatican's Council for the Laity, has warned: "There's a danger that the presence of laypeople, for example, in mass media and in politics, is not pushed enough. People need to see that their faith belongs not only in the parish but also in other areas."[2]

If it is not careful, the church by the year 2000 could find itself—with its fantastic liturgies, its comprehensive renewal programs, its well-functioning parish teams—as an end in itself and not a means for something greater.

The laity have come of age in the United States. Laypeople are better educated, wealthier, more politically powerful than any other generation of American Catholics. They hold responsible positions in government, industry, education, the military and social service. They are successful spouses and parents. They are leaders in their communities.

These laywomen and laymen are ready to accept their role in the world and are in positions where the exercise of their lay vocations can make a difference. In the post-Vatican II church the center of lay involvement must move from diocese and parish to the workplace, the family and the neighborhood.

How tragic it would be if, so soon after Vatican II, the central insight of that great Council were to be lost: The church is church precisely as it tries to make the kingdom come in the modern world.

A confident and competent laity is the key to realizing this vision.

Chapter I: Church

For God did not send his Son into the world to
be its judge, but to be its savior.

—John 3:17

More than 20 years after the Second Vatican
Council, too many laypeople still think of the church
as either the building in which they worship or the
clergy who run the institution. The Council defined
the church as the people of God. Yet in practice the
people of God are identified with those who hang
around the building and the clergy. For many
laypeople the church is still a peripheral concern,
something relegated to the realm of the sacred and
having little to do with their daily lives in the secular
world.

The church is a much broader reality than the
liturgical, educational and social programs of the
institutional church. The church is the community of
believers acting together in and to the world. Vatican
II clearly condemned any split between faith and
daily life, counting such a dichotomy "...among the

more serious errors of our age."[1] The Council charted the road to salvation directly through daily preoccupations, not in a retreat behind church walls:

> Thus, far from thinking that works produced by man's own talent and energy are in opposition to God's power . . . Christians are convinced that the triumphs of the human race are a sign of God's greatness and the flowering of His own mysterious design. . . . Hence it is clear that men are not deterred by the Christian message from building up the world, or impelled to neglect the welfare of their fellows. They are, rather, more stringently bound to do these very things.[2]

Vatican II should have ended any dualistic understanding of heaven and earth. The temporal world and the heavenly kingdom are not two separate realities, said the Council Fathers. "On this earth that kingdom is already present in mystery."[3] There is no need to endure the world as if it were merely a series of temptations or structural evils to be suffered through or overcome. New York Governor Mario Cuomo observed, "We used to look upon the world as a training ground, an obstacle course. The Council taught us that the world is good and to be built up with our activity."[4]

Not everyone shares this understanding of the role of the temporal world in eternal salvation. Many Christians—fundamentalists and others—believe that their faith sets them above or against human culture. Others think of worldly affairs as what John Courtney Murray called "basketweaving": something to fill the idle time between baptism and death. Still others, like those to whom Cuomo refers, tiptoe through the booby-trapped world of near occasions of sin, hoping to arrive at death untouched by moral ambiguity.

It is precisely the activity of sustaining and improving the world, of building the kingdom of God on earth, which Vatican II says is the primary vocation of the laity. This call is not opposed to lay participation in meeting the internal needs of the church. Rather, the needs of the church at work in the world give purpose and meaning to the liturgical, educational and social programs of the worshiping community.

The ordinary work of people on their jobs, with their families and in their neighborhoods is as much a part of the function of the church as is Sunday Mass or Tuesday evening Bible study. This daily fidelity to work sustains and improves the human community, and thus advances the kingdom of God. The confident laity trust that, over time, normal human competence creates orderly and peaceful institutions which mirror God's plan for the earth.

The church has two distinct but symbiotic functions: to be a nourishing community for its members and to sustain and improve the world. Vatican II clearly reaffirmed: "Christ's redemptive work, while of itself directed toward the salvation of men, involves also the renewal of the whole temporal order. Hence the mission of the church is not only to bring to men the message and grace of Christ, but also to penetrate and perfect the temporal sphere with the spirit of the gospel."[5]

Laypeople must recognize that they are the vanguard of the church at work in the world, penetrating and perfecting the temporal sphere. For who is the church at work in the world if not mothers, fathers, teachers, government workers, accountants, secretaries, lawyers, artists, doctors, nurses, production workers, and others? Through their unions, businesses, families, agencies, professional associations, community organizations, political parties and other secular institutions, Christians fulfill the church's obligation to sustain and improve the world.

Because of the nature of their vocations, the laity, not the clergy, are most effective as church at work in the world. Businessmen and businesswomen are most able to reform corporations. Active, dues-paying union members can best affect organized labor. Professionals must influence their own professions. Parents are ultimately responsible for their children's future. Residents will protect and promote their own communities.

Some maintain that a clergy-lay distinction is at best outdated and at worst divisive, the last remnant of the two-tiered (sacred/secular) theology rejected by Vatican II. They charge that the clergy-lay distinction is unbiblical, that in fact we are all members of the *laos*: God's people. If the purpose of the clergy-lay distinction is to prevent the laity from full participation in the liturgical life of the institutional church or to prohibit the clergy from working in the world, then these critics are obviously correct. As Richard Mouw has observed, however, "There are important differences between those who work full time as salaried employees of the institutional church and those of us who spend most of our working hours outside of that institution. These differences, as I see things, are to be neither ignored nor regretted."[6]

A better distinction than that between clergy and laity might be between the church in preparation and reflection and the church at work in the world. All Christians—clergy and laity—operate in both facets of the church some of the time. Some (mostly clergy, religious and an increasing number of lay people) are paid by the church to lead the entire community in preparation and reflection. Most (almost all the laity, and a few clergy and religious in special circumstances) earn their living in the world and spend most of their time as the church at work in the world.

These are not rigid categories. Obviously, some people paid by the church work full-time in the world: nurses at a Catholic hospital, or a housing specialist at Catholic Charities, for example. Many of those paid by the church for preparation and reflection also volunteer part of their time to the church at work in the world. Conversely, more and more laypeople with secular vocations also help the church in preparation and reflection. This interchange is healthy for the church as a whole.

It is critical, however, that distinctions and priorities be clear. The church in preparation and reflection is to serve the church in the world. Theologian John Coleman pointed out:

> The church as institution is constantly to be judged by how well it nurtures and serves the church as community of faith, because the institution, while indispensable, is always of merely instrumental value, a necessary minimum ingredient of order as the precondition for the deeper reality of freedom, variety and dynamic interaction with the world. The proper arena for forging the concrete historical ideal, then, is not within the church, but in the world.[7]

One of the most serious problems in the American Catholic church today is that too often the church in preparation and reflection has begun to treat itself as master rather than as servant of the church at work in the world. Parish and diocesan budgets, plans and programs too often deal almost exclusively with the problems of the church in preparation and reflection.

For example, at "Jesus Day IV," a daylong conference sponsored by the Office of Evangelization of the Archdiocese of Chicago and attended by over 1000 people, one of the workshops was on long-range planning for the archdiocese. The workshop leader was the priest-director of the archdiocesan planning office. He focused on only one issue, the projected decline in the number of priests, as if this were the only problem facing the archdiocese. The only solution he proposed was to train laypeople to take over more functions inside the church. No one at the workshop, although most were laypeople, objected to either the narrow focus of the subject or the exclusive solution proposed.

The *Directory of Diocesan Lay Programs and Resources* published by the American Catholic Bishops' Committee on the Laity locates many resources directed toward training lay paraprofessionals within church structures. No programs are listed which specifically help laypeople to function better in the secular world.

Many parishes around the country have begun the tradition of affirming the laity's call to service by expanding the renewal of the clergy's vows on Holy Thursday to include all in-house lay ministers. While these active laypeople gather around the altar to recite a prayer of service, the rest of the congregation is left in the pews. This liturgy clearly communicates that those laypeople who work inside the church share in the priestly ministry, and those who do not are somehow less involved Christians.

The diocese of Brooklyn held a "priestless day" in which every priest went to a day of prayer and planning about the vocation crisis. A handful of retired priests handled emergency calls for all the parishes. The day was meant to dramatize the projected shortage of priests in the diocese. No such work-stoppage has been held to highlight the vocation crises for school teachers, community organizers, nurses, parents or others struggling with the meaning of their work and the availability of resources to accomplish their goals.

There is nothing wrong with the church worrying about the decline in the number of priests. It is not healthy for the laity, however, to get distracted by the clerical shortage to the detriment of their own vocation in and to the world. The church at work in the world is in just as deep a crisis as the church in preparation and reflection. There is a tremendous need for programs to support laypeople in their vocations to job, family and neighborhood. The church must recognize itself as a means for directing and supporting its members to effective external purposes.

Clarification of the vocation of the laity at work in the world can also yield a new understanding of the church in preparation and reflection and therefore an accompanying appreciation of the proper role of the clergy and laity in exercising that function. To better support the diverse vocations of the church at work in the world, the church in preparation and reflection will have to become much more competent in organizational and management skills. Rather than being solely responsible for job, family and neighborhood problems of church members, the church in preparation and reflection must learn how to encourage and empower laypeople to solve their own individual and societal problems.

It is only when the church at work in the world is recognized and celebrated equally with the church in preparation and reflection that the two functions of the church will be mutually supportive.

Laypeople, whose primary work is in the world, know instinctually that their experience, concerns and vocations are different from most clergy and those laypeople primarily concerned with the internal functioning of the church. To ignore or deny this difference is to create a false unity and to lose the dynamic of the church as the mystical body of Christ, with various parts and functions.

A confident laity cannot afford to lose the truth behind the distinction between the church in preparation and reflection and the church at work in the world. Laypeople must develop a sense of their own vocation. Otherwise, their only notion of church will be "churchy" involvement. They will see ministry and vocation as something special, something for priests, sisters and a very few laypeople. They will fail to associate the bulk of their time on the job, with their family and in their neighborhood with being church.

Questions For Discussion

1) What is your understanding of the institutional church? Do you have a broader concept of "church" that extends beyond this institutional structure?

2) Is the message of Christianity part of your daily life? What are the ways in which your parish might affirm your work in the world?

3) Do you see ways in which lay people can undertake the Vatican II mandate to bring about the kingdom of God on earth through their work in the world?

4) What is your understanding of the authors' distinction between the church in preparation and reflection and the church at work in the world? How can these two functions cooperate as one church?

Chapter II: Vocation

But you are a chosen race, the King's priests, the holy nation, God's own people, chosen to proclaim the wonderful acts of God, who called you out of darkness into his own marvelous light.

—1 Peter 2:9

The clerical vocation shortage presents both an opportunity and a threat to the post Vatican II, lay-centered church. The opportunity is a recognition of the great outpouring of gifts among all God's people for service inside the church. The threat is a deceptive narrowing of the church's vision that allows the enthusiasm for internal ministries to divert the church from its challenge to sustain and improve the world.

If they are to be the church at work in the world, laypeople need to understand that their vocation is as real as any bishop's, priest's, sister's or brother's. Through baptism Christians are called to service, to ministry, to the task of building up the kingdom of God on earth.

Before Vatican II the mission of the church seemed to be the exclusive responsibility of the clergy with a minor assist from "the good nuns." Laity were the sheep, who docilely followed their shepherds. To be a layperson was often to define oneself as non-clergy in the context of an institutional, liturgical, sacramental, religious organization. The Council reminded the faithful that they are members of the baptized priesthood: "The baptized, by regeneration and the anointing of the Holy Spirit, are consecrated into a spiritual house and a holy priesthood."[1]

This realization has made a radical difference in the internal operation of the church. It has led to the development of a whole field called lay ministry. Laypeople are now involved in various phases of liturgical celebration: reading, distributing communion and, in a few welcome experiments, preaching. Laity are also involved in explicitly church-sponsored ministries to the aged and dying; the homeless, sick or disabled; those in need of religious education; engaged, married and divorced couples; parents and their children. In fact, not one church ministry does not actively involve the laity.

Most parishes now have some form of parish council or advisory committee to the pastor. An unprecedented number of laypeople now work directly for church agencies.

Several organizations and institutes have been formed to assist the laity in fulfilling these ministries. Conferences, publications and articles galore deal with the support of lay ministers. Lay ministry is a growth industry. As Russell Barta has maintained, "This explosion of lay ministry in the American Church is an exciting development and Catholic identity is being changed in the process."[2]

Yet Barta, first president of the National Center for the Laity, and others have warned that the concept of lay ministry has an underside which—if unrecognized and not addressed—could have a long-term negative effect on the development of a confident laity.

The danger of increased lay involvement in church ministry is a kind of "paraclericalization." If the primacy of their daily vocation in and to the world is not recognized, laypeople can easily become overly concerned about the internal functioning of the church in preparation and reflection. They can also overemphasize the heroic or prophetic forms of ministry and social justice efforts organized under formal church auspices, to the neglect of their ordinary work on the job, with the family and in the neighborhood.

For most parishes and dioceses, the pressures of maintaining numerous physical plants while attending to the normal sacramental, educational and corporal demands of their members make internal lay ministry seem like the number one priority. Post-conciliar efforts to encourage lay involvement have often centered around laypeople's greater participation in the internal functioning of the church—roles and functions formerly performed predominantly by clerics. While lip service is always paid to concern for the world, it is too often made a secondary consideration—something to be done if time, energy and money are left after all the internal needs are fulfilled, usually organized and run as part of the internal church program itself.

The pastor of a large parish in Brooklyn announced that the newly assigned assistant pastor had taken ill and would not be available for months. "This is your church, not mine," the pastor told the congregation. "If you want the parish programs to continue, then it is up to you to lead them."

A true and healthy sentiment, to be sure. The pastor, however, erred by omission. His error was in indentifying lay involvement exclusively with church-related programs. He forgot to mention that such lay ministry to the parish only makes sense after responsibilities to family, job and neighborhood have been met, and that such responsibilities are as much about being called as any of the parish programs.

As Ed Marciniak lamented:

> What bedevils our pastoral theology and existing practice is the mind-set that automatically expects a lay person who is deeply committed to Jesus Christ to become a paracleric in the Church's civil service as a mini-priest or mini-sister. . . . The U.S. church has chosen to allocate staff and budgets to train its paraprofessionals. One searches in vain for programs that enable the lay people to better understand the Christian service of the working life.[3]

Time, money and energy are spent training the laity as eucharistic ministers, parish council members, liturgists, religious education directors, social service workers and the like. The lay diaconate is reinstituted and other lay ministries in the church are created, acknowledged, blessed and celebrated. All of this activity creates the impression—despite the best of intentions of those promoting them—that the laity best fulfill their baptismal mission by being involved in internal church functions rather than being involved in the daily world of work.

While being careful not to pit the church in preparation and reflection against the church at work in the world, Bishop James Hoffman, the former chairman of the U.S. Catholic Bishops' Committee on the Laity, admitted:

> We seem to have placed greater value upon ministry within the church and perhaps by default have disvalued the crucial work of lay women and men in the world. It is my personal conviction that we need to attend to that vision of the Second Vatican Council relative to the lay apostolate and to provide support and encouragement for those who spend their lives in the crucial secular occupations, be it politics, communications, science, whatever.[4]

Since Vatican II, involvement of the laity has largely been assumed to be an internal affair. The laity minister to the needs of the church in preparation and reflection. Many laypeople themselves feel that they are not involved Christians if they do not take part in this internal ministry.

"I am not formally involved in any lay programs these days," wrote a professor at a major university. "Professional demands are such that my work has to be my arena of service outside of the family. Apart from that, both my wife and I feel we should get involved in party politics at the local level."

This Christian has captured the essence of being a layperson, but because lay involvement has become synonymous with internal church ministry he feels guilty about his distance from parish lay ministry.

A woman in a workshop on ministry apologized: "You see, I've never had time to do ministry. . . . I've never had time to do Altar Guild, teach the children in the school." This woman was startled to realize that ministry included her work in the world: "You mean looking after my mother for the last 20 years is part of my ministry?"[5]

Part of the problem, of course, is semantic. Some try to distinguish ministry from vocation. Others try to decide if there is one vocation, two vocations or as many vocations as there are jobs and ministries. This confusion and theological speculation may be necessary for a time, but it is not very helpful to a confident laity. For our purposes we will limit the definition of ministry to Christian service connected with the institutional church in preparation and reflection.

Not all laypeople, then, are called to ministry. All Christians should recognize, however, that they have a vocation, or calling, to Christian service, which can be carried out in a variety of ways and situations. There is a vocation to homemaking, teaching, building construction, firefighting, nursing, art, and many other occupations. One legitimate way of serving is certainly in institutional church programs. But that is not the only way.

Unfortunately, too often people think of vocation only in terms of the explicitly religious life—priests, sisters and brothers. In its special vocations issue, a California diocesan paper explained the distinction between clerical vocations and the vocations of all the baptized:

> Each of us, as baptized Christians, is called to minister to each other and to the mission of building up the body of Christ. Church Vocations Awareness Week celebrates this universal call to love and service. The week can be one of prayer, education and action about vocations, especially to the priesthood and religious life. Each individual is urged to a deeper appreciation of his/her own vocation.[6]

This balance, minimal as it was, between clerical and worldly vocations, did not extend through the rest of the issue itself, however, where there were the predictable stories about the priestly and religious life. Rarely does writing on vocations include any discussion of the vocation to lay occupations. If the church in preparation and reflection is to remain credible in the eyes of the laity it must broaden its perspective on vocation.

Even when it comes to involvement in secular affairs, the emphasis on church-based lay ministry has carried over to the manner in which laity are encouraged to work in the world. Laypeople are not taught that their normal work in the world—on their job, with their family, in their neighborhood—is the usual locus of their ministry or vocation. Rather, the notion is being advanced that only out of the ordinary and usually church-related witness is social ministry or social action.

This means that in order to be the church at work in the world, laypeople have to "do" social ministry. Usually, this means joining a church-related social justice group. What Mark Gibbs observed in the Anglican church is no less true in the Roman Catholic: "If there is to be any social action, the best way to do it is to form or support a parish group. . . . There is little mention of other civic or professional voluntary groups, and even less about witnessing in the present structures of secular society, where the laity are week by week."[7]

Too often laypeople are given the impression that if they do not join the parish social justice committee, they do not, or cannot, do social justice. If they are not members of the St. Vincent de Paul Society, they have no ministry to the poor. If they do not visit the sick or the imprisoned through the parish hospital or prison ministries, they have no opportunity to perform those corporal works of mercy.

Part of the impression this "extra-ordinarization" of lay ministry has created is that only prophetic action on behalf of social justice fulfills the

Vatican II understanding of the church in the modern world. The day-to-day concerns and actions of the average layperson are equated with materialism and selfishness, or at best perceived as ineffective or merely the exercise of individual ethics. The ability of people to sustain and improve the world through their own individual or combined efforts outside of church auspices is hardly recognized.

Perhaps a story will help clarify this point:

In January 1984 a fire totally destroyed the Allen-Edmonds shoe factory in Belgium, Wisconsin. It looked as though the 250 employees of that firm would permanently lose their jobs, spelling economic disaster for the small town. Instead, Allen-Edmonds president John Stollenwerk was able to run a pun in the newspaper within a couple of days: "We'll be back on your feet in no time."

What made Stollenwerk's advertisement possible was an act of generosity from his competitor, Robert Laverenz of Laverenz Shoe Company in nearby Sheboygan, Wisconsin. "It wasn't a question of should we or shouldn't we help out," said Laverenz. "The question was how soon and how much could we help."

Laverenz huddled with members of Local 796 of the United Food and Commercial Workers, the union for his employees. They called a meeting of their fellow workers at Laverenz Shoe Co. and voted to switch to a four day work week. "Every single hand went up in affirmation," Laverenz said in praise. When Laverenz Shoe Company closed at 4:30 on Thursday, the Allen-Edmonds employees arrived on a bus. They produced 1,200 pairs of shoes a week for their company by working continuous shifts through the weekends.

There was no formal church or parish involvement in this act of sustaining and improving the world, no prophetic actions, no special ministries—just laypeople collectively doing what they thought was right in the normal course of their lives.

If the church in preparation and reflection continues to overemphasize lay ministries in, to and through itself, the vocation of the church at work in the world will be lost. For while the need is great inside the church, it is much greater in the world. And while the gifts of many laypeople can certainly be used by the church in preparation and reflection, they are needed much more by the church at work in the world. By making laypeople into paraclerics, the church turns inward upon itself. By insisting on extraordinary activity as the only valid form of work in the world, the church takes laypeople away from the means and arena of action that is most easily accessible to them. Such a tendency prevents a confident laity from understanding and practicing its own spirituality.

The church in preparation and reflection has the responsibility to train, support, agitate and minister to this church at work in the world. An inverted vision that has the church in action spending all of its time ministering under the auspices of the church in preparation and reflection runs counter to what it means to be a Catholic in the United States in the 20th century.

Questions For Discussion

1) How do you understand your vocation as a layperson? Does seeing your work in the world as a call from God to Christian service change your attitude toward that work?

2) Do you see the understanding and vision of church changing as a result of the priest shortage or will paraclericalization merely bring about a replacement of ordained by lay ministers?

3) Can lay ministries within the church grow out of and then reach back into a person's daily life in the world? Can external and internal ministries be complementary rather than mutually exclusive?

4) How can a vocation to Christian service be carried out in your daily life without being part of recognized church structures?

Chapter III: Spirituality of Work

So God created human beings, making them to be like himself. He created them male and female, blessed them, and said, "Have many children, so that your descendants will live all over the earth and bring it under their control."

—*Genesis 1:27-28*

Laypeople must realize that their daily work is the primary means by which they help bring about the kingdom of God. Any spirituality which detracts or distracts from work is therefore counter-productive.

In the final sentences of his encyclical *On Human Work*, Pope John Paul II wrote: "Let the Christian who listens to the living word of God, uniting work with prayer, know the place his work has not only in earthly progress but also in *the development of the kingdom of God*, to which we are all called through the power of the Holy Spirit and through the word of the gospel."[1]

There are two important ideas in the pope's teaching on work. First, he elevates work united with prayer to a key place in both the temporal world and the kingdom of God. Work is not mere toil. It is not the punishment for Adam and Eve's sin, but rather an essential element in salvation. Work contributes not only to material well-being but also to the holy kingdom of God.

Second, since we are all called to work in the process of building the kingdom, then work cannot be limited merely to paid employment. All activity which helps build the kingdom is work: on the job, with the family, and in the community. And the value of all work is to be judged not by its monetary remuneration but by its contribution to building the kingdom.

According to Vatican II work refers to any human activity that cooperates with God's ongoing creation: "Throughout the course of centuries men have labored to better the circumstances of their lives through a monumental amount of individual and collective effort. To believers, this point is settled: *considered in itself* such human activity accords with God's will. For man, created to God's image, received a mandate to subject to himself the earth and all that it contains" (authors' emphasis).[2]

John Paul II has this wider notion of work in mind when he calls it "a fundamental dimension of man's existence on earth."[3] Worship, sacraments and devotions are important for preparation and reflection, but the mandate of Christianity is the work of building the kingdom.

Because of his broad understanding of human work, John Paul II can refer to the basic Christian way as a "spirituality of work."[4] This phrase at first sounds strange to those who equate spirituality with pious devotions. But work contains the key to a complete and fulfilling spirituality.

Daily work can unite the sacred and the secular in genuine Christian spirituality. Such a spirituality requires that the world be regarded as a proper home to be sustained, improved and completed. The older view of the world as a source of trial and temptation, as an obstacle course to be overcome, must be replaced by one that sees the world as an incarnation of the love of God.

A spirituality of work also demands blurring the distinction between the church and the world. The church is no longer a spiritual refuge from the evil world but is rather involved daily in the process of creating the world in the image of God.

Finally, a spirituality of work means that there must be a new definition of spirituality for laypeople involved in the world. Rather than implying overtly religious acts, spirituality should refer to the integration of faith into the concrete circumstances of a person's life.

Once spirituality comes to mean not only the way a Christian prays, but more completely the way one comes to God through occupational, family and neighborhood responsibilities, then the phrase "spirituality of work" no longer sounds so strange.

At the heart of a work-centered spirituality is the relationship between the perfection of things and institutions on the one hand and the perfection of human beings on the other. The first aim of work is to bring creation toward perfection. If one's work entails production of physical objects, then it means building the best objects possible: spacecraft launchers, automobiles, books, works of art. If one's work is service, then those services must be brought to successful completion: administering therapy, serving a meal, giving a lecture, or finishing the family laundry. If one is responsible for the institutions of society, then work entails making those institutions responsive: by serving on a community board, voting in an election, writing a letter to an editor, participating in a union or a professional association.

The second aim of work, however, is the completion, harmonization, and realization of the worker. The perfection of creation must include the perfection of the person doing the work. To finish a job, to do work well, to bring things into perfection, takes more than technical skill. It takes a sense of ownership of the work being performed, a pride in its execution, and a recognition of its value.

Good work requires a respect for its own strict and binding rules. Space exploration, for example, has its own inner rules which, if not respected, will cause destruction—despite the best intentions of the workers—as demonstrated by the space shuttle Challenger tragedy. This interior virtue allows work to come naturally to the worker.

When both of the major aims of work, the product and the producer, are in harmony, a spirituality of work is possible. Spirituality is the way people discipline themselves toward the divine. The church at work in the world can have a spirituality uniquely its own, based on immersion in, rather than withdrawal from, the world.

The first challenge of a spirituality of work is the integration of the three components of each person's work: job, family and neighborhood. Such integration is not a matter of spending an equal amount of time in each area. Rather, it creates a wholeness, or holiness, about work. Laypeople know that they are the same people on the job as they are with the family and around the neighborhood. The same man who makes a real effort to treat his wife as an equal and raise his children to be respectful must also promote the same atmosphere on his job and in community affairs. Failure to do so causes an internal conflict which is a barrier to spiritual growth. His actions in daily life validate or negate his spirituality.

A spirituality of work presents a second challenge for it must be developed in the daily world of mixed motives. Such a spirituality is more difficult than a retreat from the world but at the same time it is more accessible to the average layperson. One worker observed: "Sometimes I see my work as creative and redemptive, but usually I'm thinking about my paycheck." In order to develop a spirituality of work, this layperson must understand that the basic economic motive in no way distorts the creative and redemptive dimensions of working. The recognition and balancing of motives provides the basis for a spirituality of work.

The third challenge of a spirituality of work is competency. "If a man is called to be a streetsweeper," Martin Luther King, Jr. often said, "he should sweep streets even as Michelangelo painted, or Beethoven composed music, or Shakespeare wrote poetry. He should sweep streets so well that all the host of heaven and earth will pause to say 'here lived a great streetsweeper who did his job well.' "[5] Any notion that good intentions can somehow spiritualize shoddy work must be rejected. John Paul II contradicted such tendencies in an address to businesspeople and industrial workers in Barcelona: "We all have the duty to do our work well. If we wish to realize ourselves properly, we may not avoid our duty or perform our work in a mediocre way, without interest, just to get it over with."[6] Confident laypeople, doing what they are supposed to be doing and doing it well, are as holy as any monk on a mount. A plumber doing a job with skill and conscientiousness, parents putting their children through school, community leaders protecting the value of their neighborhoods—these are the church at work in the world pursuing their spirituality.

A spirituality of work also challenges the church in preparation and reflection. The models of spirituality that have been explored and celebrated by the church in the past have been basically monastic. Such spirituality implies a view of the active lay life as secular or non-religious. Most spiritual programs propose that a person step back, at least for awhile, from family, job and community obligations.

Teilhard de Chardin described the prevalent attitude toward spirituality:

> I don't think I am exaggerating when I say that nine out of ten practicing Christians feel that man's work is always at the level of a spiritual encumbrance. In spite of the practice of right intentions, and the day offered every morning to God, the general run of the faithful dimly feel that the time spent at the office or the studio, in the fields or in the factory, is time spent away from prayer and adoration.[7]

Until now, laypeople have not had much help in seeing any part of their work as a spiritual experience. If laypeople cannot find any spiritual meaning in their work, they are condemned to living a certain dual life: not connecting what they do on Sunday morning with what they do the rest of the week. They need to discover that the very actions of daily life are spiritual and enable laypeople to touch God *in* the world, not away from it. Such a spirituality will say to the layperson worried about lack of time for prayer: "Your work is your prayer."

The challenge for a confident laity is to fashion

this spirituality out of the ordinary language of daily life. Most workers, for example, cannot readily articulate the overall meaning of their work. The language in which they learned their trade and in which they conduct daily business is not given to speaking about creation, salvation, the common good and the transformation of the world. Instead, the language of the marketplace is mired in individualism, competition and materialism. Students contemplating a career are not in an environment in which choices are made using language like vocation, discerning one's gifts and contributing to the commonweal. Most will embark on a career based on the luck or circumstance of finding their first job. Within a short time, these young workers often find that the individualistic parlance does not provide answers to life's deeper questions. They will discover that adult moral life is less a matter of ethics than a search for the *meaning* of family, social and economic life.

In the lifelong grappling with the meaning of work in the light of faith, aided by the church in preparation and reflection, most laity will discover the spiritual dimensions of their lives. This discovery will happen in many ways but laypeople themselves will have to take the initiative, gathering to reflect together on the meaning of their work.

There are already some beginning efforts to link faith and work. These support programs, however, are only a first step toward an integrated spirituality of work. The world-sustaining and -improving dimension of these programs often gets lost in the process of maintaining the mutually supportive small communities they create.

Prominent among the parish-based renewal programs are RENEW, found in 5,000 of the 19,000 parishes in the United States, and Christ Renews His Parish, found in another 400 parishes. These programs encourage the laity to connect faith and daily life.

The Cursillo movement is another major support network. After making a three-day retreat, *cursillistas* are urged to meet regularly in small groups for short prayers, reflections on piety, spiritual reading, and discussion of "apostolic successes and failures in work, family and environment."

Marriage Encounter and the Christian Family Movement seek to focus on the laity's role inside the family.

Other support movements and loosely-formed small groups follow these general models. Members take turns hosting home gatherings that are structured so that certain elements are always present: prayer, sharing of important events around the home and workplace, and a discussion of reading material.

Some centers try to support the spiritual significance of certain professions. The Boston Labor Guild is among the last remaining Catholic labor schools in the United States. Over 1000 women and men who are trying to apply the principles of

Christianity to their work in labor-management relations belong to the Guild. They attend adult education classes in the areas of labor history, parliamentary procedure, social ethics and affirmative action. The Guild also appreciates the world-improving dimension of faith. Its annual awards program honors those who reorder and humanize institutions from the inside, in accord with social justice. "These men and women," says the Guild, "daily wrestle with the problems of good order and justice in a continually shifting arena of employment relations. . . . Their vocation addresses the promotion and maintenance of orderly justice and dignity in the workplaces of this Commonwealth."[8]

The Institute for Theological Encounter with Science and Technology in St. Louis helps its members grapple with the meaning of being Christian in light of the rapid advances in genetics, computers, nuclear physics, and so on. For the past 16 years, the Institute has been building a community of scientists dedicated to both the advancement of scientific and technological development and the support of Christianity in the world.

Some laypeople have taken the initiative to form support groups unrelated to any national movement or specific profession. A Washington, D.C. support group includes a homemaker, a journalist, a White House staff member, an urban economist and a government planner. They have met regularly for over five years to share experiences in applying Christian values to everyday life, to give each other support, and to pray.

A group of small-business owners in Hartford, Connecticut, meets every month to talk about how to make their shops more human places to work. They also discuss general problems in the business community: layoffs, housing and employment.

Even groups of unemployed Christians are meeting for mutual support and shared prayer in places like Rochester, New York; Orland Park, Illinois; and Cleveland, Ohio.

Some retreat programs are being developed which address a spirituality of work. Market Place Ministries is one such effort. Developed in Canada, it aims at supporting busy laypeople in their civil responsibilities. The Council of Catholic Men/Holy Name of Chicago has sponsored two very successful "Men Ministering to Men" retreats, during which the men became more attuned to naming the activity of God in their work world. Some parishes have used "The Supper Table" retreat developed by Washington's Center of Concern to try to link faith and work.

Even taken together and with hundreds of other initiatives currently happening around the country, all these efforts have touched only a minority of American Catholics. Until the church in preparation and reflection, with all of its institutional strength, focuses on the vocation of the laity in and to the world, a spirituality of work will continue to be an idea whose time has not yet come.

When laypeople begin to realize that their spirituality is found through their work on the job, with their families and in their neighborhoods, they will assume their proper place as the church at work in the world with competence and confidence. Then the exit signs inside our church buildings will read: "Now entering the mission field. Return when you need reinforcements."

Questions For Discussion

1) How can your daily work be a genuine form of Christian spirituality? Is this a way to "pray always," as Paul told the Ephesians?

2) How does a "spirituality of work" change your view of the world and how can it improve the quality of your work?

3) What is your understanding of the wholeness or holiness that a spirituality of work can bring to the lives of laypeople?

Chapter IV: Self-Interest

When people criticize me, this is how I defend myself: Don't I have the right to be given food and drink for my work? Don't I have the right to follow the example of the other apostles and the Lord's brothers and Peter, by taking a Christian wife with me on my trips?

—*1 Corinthians 9:3-5*

In developing their own spirituality, confident, competent laypeople must act in a complex world of jobs, families and neighborhoods, a world that is neither a garden of pure good nor a bottomless pit of evil. Choices are seldom made between absolute good and total evil; more often they are made among conflicting goods. The right thing sometimes gets done for the wrong reason. Other times the wrong thing gets done out of good intentions.

Any road to holiness for the layperson must wind around the twists and bends of mixed motives. And if the church in preparation and reflection is to be truly helpful to the church at work in the world, then it must help the laity deal with its day-to-day experience.

Vatican II recognized mixed motives. The Council teaches that work is a participation in God's work, "even the most ordinary everyday activities. For while providing the substance of life for themselves and their families, men and women are performing their activities in a way which appropriately benefits society."[1]

We encounter mixed motives in most of our actions. A college student may volunteer to help feed 300 homeless people on Thanksgiving. He knows that a woman he likes from the Newman club might also volunteer. He also knows that he has to write a sociology term paper and that this volunteer effort may give him some data. Some physical labor will help him forget that his deceased father will not be around for his own Thanksgiving meal later in the day.

None of these motives diminishes the student's act of kindness. All the others who volunteered part of their holiday to help feed the hungry—the social worker, the boy scout, the juvenile officer, the senior citizen—have a variety of motives for doing what they do.

A dilemma arises when the church in preparation and reflection implies that purely motivated, heroic action is the essence of Christianity. Mother Teresa of Calcutta, for example, is an inspiration and a challenge to every Christian. But not every Christian can do as she has done—they are neither called nor equipped to do so. Few can give up their jobs, or choose not to have families, or subject their loved ones to voluntary poverty in order to give a prophetic witness to the gospel. They must live the gospel in the performance of ordinary Christian acts of kindness, and do so among the ambiguities, the compromises and the moral dilemmas of ordinary existence.

Too often laypeople feel a sense of inadequacy about the moral choices they must make. Condemnations of materialism and exhortations toward asceticism, for example, can confuse parents who are trying to provide a comfortable life for themselves and their children. The teaching of the "preferential option for the poor" discourages those laypeople who are following a middle-class road to sanctity. Their concern for their own well-being does not mean that Christians cannot be far more generous or compassionate than they usually are, nor that every Christian is not called upon many times to make basic value choices. It means that people must normally act on a mix of sometimes conflicting values.

A worker at a nuclear weapons assembly plant, for example, may be earning an income for her family. The money she earns goes to pay her taxes, support her church and charities, and, primarily, raise her children. One of her children might be handicapped and require special care. Two kids might be nearing college age. Her husband might be dead, or unemployed. She might be divorced.

She certainly has seen the devastating effects of unemployment. Perhaps the plant has threatened to leave the community, which has few other major employers. Her friends work at the plant. It is close to her home, thus enabling her to spend more time with her family. She may also get a certain amount of psychological satisfaction from her job.

This woman may be ambivalent about the morality of nuclear weapons, or even see them as a deterrent to war. Part of her work may have peaceful applications.

If the church in preparation and reflection, in the person of the bishop, for example, calls on workers at the plant to examine their consciences regarding their jobs, it is right and proper for this woman to do so. Being a faithful Christian and a mature laywoman, she will consider what the bishop is saying in light of the conflicts among all the values in her life.

She might decide to take a radical, prophetic stand and quit her job. She might decide that the other factors in her life preclude her making any changes. She might decide to compromise in some way by taking a retraining course to prepare herself for another career, by planning a move to another city three years hence, by supporting a peace group, by joining a civic organization committed to retooling defense industries for peaceful production.

Any of these may or may not be the most moral thing to do. As a confident, competent laywoman, she will realize she is experiencing value conflicts. After prayer and reflection, she will decide upon a course of action.

Laypeople face these kinds of decisions every day. While it is perfectly fine for the church in preparation and reflection to hold up ideals, it is also the duty of that same church to help people handle the ambiguity such ideals produce.

The key to handling this ambiguity, to unlocking the spirituality of normal Christian living, is to understand self-interest. Self-interest is the proper attention to one's own interests *in the context of the interests of others*, the instinct to protect our *legitimate* needs and desires while respecting those of others.

Self-interest is a social principle that must be negotiated in the context of a society or community. It requires division of labor, interpersonal contact and shared responsibilities. It puts actions in the reciprocal context of give and take. Self-interest, therefore, regulates the mixed motives out of which every choice is made.

To pursue our self-interest is not to be selfish. Selfishness is the *exclusive* regard for ourselves, a point of view fixed solely on our own private advantage. Selfishness is clearly evil and ultimately self-destructive. Selfish individuals do not need to deal with the needs of others because they do not intend their behavior to have any social ramifications. They are not concerned with building an institution or even social approbation.

Self-interest, however, makes people responsive to one another. It is the dynamic of society. In a pluralistic society, people cannot get what they want or need by being selfish. In the pursuit of their self-interest, they immediately come up against other people's legitimate but possibly conflicting self-interests. The only possibility for a truly just society is for all to clarify their motives and set priorities for their wants and needs, and then negotiate their self-interests with those of others. The operative principle should be the greatest good for oneself and others, the least evil on all sides and the understanding that the right thing can be done for many reasons.

One often hears that good Christians should always consider the common welfare *before* their own interests. Reinhold Niebuhr once addressed this belief by asserting: "To set self-interest and the general welfare in simple opposition is to ignore nine-tenths of the ethical issues that confront the consciences of men. For these are concerned not so much with the problem of the self against the whole as with the problems of the self in relation to the various types of general welfare."[2]

Self-interest provides a basis for operating in the public arena because it frames moral decisions in the public language of power and compromise. Moral behavior is almost never a detached, private choice between absolute good or absolute evil. Moral decision-making usually means weighing the conflicting claims or interests of many people and groups. Self-interest, because of its public, reciprocal nature, forces people to compromise.

Andrew Greeley observed:

> To compromise, then, means to settle for less than absolute morality and legitimate rights. . . . We must remember not to destroy our opponents' fundamental self-interest. . . . What is superior in pure theory is not necessarily and inevitably superior in the complex and ambiguous world of reality. . . . What is morally superior is not that which is theoretically most desirable but that which comes closest to the desired goal without doing more harm than good. . . . Modest victory is almost always the only alternative to certain defeat.[3]

Current American industrial policy is full of examples of the failure to understand conflicting self-interests.

The management of a steel-castings firm decided that five percent of the employees had to be laid off in order to keep the firm operating successfully. The public relations department was instructed to cover up the planned layoff. Such stonewalling only fueled the rumor mill. The union was projecting a 20 percent layoff; gossip had the firm moving to South America. Worker morale naturally dropped, productivity plunged, orders declined. Other businesses in the community suffered from consumer caution. The firm has now laid off 25 percent of its employees and verges on bankruptcy. The town is suffering a major recession.

"A firm committed to greed," wrote Michael Novak, "unleashes social forces that will sooner or later destroy it."[4] It would have been in the self-interest of the management of this firm to honestly disclose its situation and try to deal with the self-interests of the employees, the customers and the community. The selfish attempt to conceal the facts doomed the firm.

Yet the financial crisis was real; a layoff of some employees was necessary. Management could not keep workers employed when there was not enough business without abdicating their responsibilities. The union's job was to keep as many of its members employed as possible. The challenge in a situation like this is to get all parties to pool their ideas and resources to find a realizable solution that served everyone's needs. This cannot be done unless everyone understands and acts out of self-interest.

The virtuous exercise of self-interest allows a confident laity to function in the real world. Those who deny or denounce self-interest will forever hold out for a purity of motive unattainable in this life. Unfortunately the church in preparation and reflection correctly condemns selfishness but rarely encourages the proper understanding of self-interest. Because of this neglect, the church at work in the world often feels surprised and even guilty when it experiences mixed motives in daily life.

Instead of denigrating the real material concerns of its members, the church in preparation and reflection should be promoting those virtues that address money: ambition, humility, stewardship, responsibility, thrift, honesty and benevolence.

A silence about or disdain for self-interest contradicts everything that the church at work in the world encounters daily. This contradiction is the primary reason for the dichotomy Christians feel between their faith and their daily lives. A church in preparation and reflection that ignores the everyday realities of the church at work in the world relegates itself to Sunday morning irrelevance. Rather than deny or degrade self-interest, the church in preparation and reflection would do better to celebrate the exercise of Christian self-interest by emphasizing the moral formation of the self. Is it a selfish self or a generous self? Is it a self that recognizes that true self-interest entails the welfare of others, notably the poor?

Confident laity know that legitimate conflict among competing ideas, ideals and moralities is inevitable. One cannot convince other parties to relinquish their self-interests because of the moral superiority of one's own positions. To the extent that all interests are respected, moral solutions will be constructed. Sooner or later every emerging interest must subordinate part of its interests to the interests of others.

By clearly acknowledging the various self-interests at stake in society, the church in preparation and reflection might have greater success in expanding people's moral horizons. Many church activists complain that people are apathetic: "You can get them motivated for a little while but then they get distracted by the concerns of their daily lives."

The solution is rather for activists to listen for

people's concerns and self-interests. To talk to people about national and international issues of peace and justice when they are worried about feeding their families, about their working conditions, about the deterioration of their own neighborhoods, merely contributes to the sense of pressure experienced by so many well-meaning Christians.

"But," the church activists will say, "we cannot wait for people to see the importance of the world situation. Even if the average person does not understand how problems in other areas affect him or her, they do. In fact, their self-interest is at stake."

This may be very true, but it is a fact of human nature that one must start with people where they are, not where one wants them to be. People are concerned with their perceived self-interest, and if their self-interest is not respected then few people are going to spend a substantial amount of time or energy trying to help others. "Maybe by arguing self-interest," said Mario Cuomo, "we can teach the good uses of compassion. . . . Helping the poor and disadvantaged and those who need a lot of help makes good common sense."[5]

At a parish discussion of the bishops' pastoral on the economy, a middle-aged businessman burst out: "There's no sense talking about morality and the economic life. If you have any doubts, I'm here as living proof. I operate out of greed all day." Here was a graced moment. This man had come to be converted, but it was critical that the group understand self-interest. If the man were scolded or preached to, he would leave as he came. His trip would have been a confession but there would have been no conversion. If this man's legitimate self-interest, mixed motives and value conflicts could be understood and accepted, however, then he could be moved to become an agent for social justice. The prudent courage he might execute in his business might set an example and formulate a policy with wide implications.

It is through the acceptance and use of self-interest that a confident laity can fulfill its vocation to bring about the kingdom of God on earth and can truly exercise the virtue of social justice.

Questions For Discussion

1) Select one or two important choices you have made in your life, and carefully reflect on your motives for these choices. Weren't all the motives in keeping with gospel values? Why did you choose as you did?

2) What is the meaning of *altruism*? How does this relate to the concept of self-interest? Can altruism conflict with self-interest? If so, how?

Chapter V:
Social Justice

There will be no more death, no more grief or crying or pain. The old things have disappeared.

—Revelation 21:4

Social justice is not a matter of individual morality, nor is it the exercise of individual charity. These are necessary just to make the world liveable. Social justice transforms the world and helps bring about the kingdom of God on earth.

Social justice is about effecting improvements, not forming committees, taking stands or issuing statements. Through social justice the institutions of society are structured to be more responsive to human needs.

The object of social justice is improved institutions, not better individuals. As Vatican II taught: "It grows increasingly true that the obligations of justice and love are fulfilled only if each person, contributing to the common good according to his own abilities and the needs of others, also promotes and assists the public and private institutions dedicated to bettering the conditions of human life."[1]

It is simply too much to expect an individual to be just in every transaction. "On the whole," said George Orwell, "human beings want to be good, but not too good, and not quite all the time."[2] Each moral act is conditioned by one's environment, and good environment supports virtue. A society is called good because of its good social habits, its institutions. As a theory of individual justice needs to appreciate individual habits, a theory of social justice needs to appreciate social habits.

Religious institutions aren't the only ones that promote virtue. All institutions that conform to justice are sources of grace. They do not have to be explicitly Christian institutions, nor do any of the members of the institution have to proclaim their faith publicly. Those who maintain good institutions by doing their work competently are *ipso facto* contributing to social justice.

Conversely institutions can become so far removed from the purpose of advancing humankind that they can metaphorically be sinful; the people who support those institutions also sin. The challenge of social justice is to reform or replace such institutions. This can sometimes be done in a radical, prophetic manner. It can as often be done by those inside the institutions themselves.

The practice of social justice can be out of the ordinary. One immediately thinks of such modern

American religious activists as Molly Rush, Mitch Snyder and Martin Luther King, Jr. Social justice can also be performed under the auspices of the institutional church: the pro-life campaign, the sanctuary movement, some aspects of the civil rights movement.

But the very fact that the church in preparation and reflection only extols these extraordinary examples confuses the laity and implies that there is no *ordinary* form of social justice. The ordinary practice of social justice needs clarification and proposition.

The term social justice has gained wide currency in the church in preparation and reflection in the last 20 years. A few years ago the few Catholics talking about social justice obtained a national reputation. Today a social justice committee is associated with almost every parish and diocese in the country, with little observable increase in effective practice of the virtue.

Most renewal and educational programs sponsored by the church in preparation and reflection include a social justice component. The Archdiocese of Chicago sponsors a lay ministry training program with three parts: interpersonal, theological and organizational skills training. Social justice is taught during the organizational trimester.

A vice-president of a large Chicago bank, a graduate of the lay ministry program, taught one of the organizational trimesters. He presented social justice through a long, hypothetical case study of a parish's efforts to close a porno movie theater in its neighborhood. The lay ministry instructor concluded by urging his students to start social concerns committees in their parish to tackle other such situations, thereby, promoting social justice. Those attending the seminar were left with the distinct impression that social justice is about starting another parish committee.

What if the banker had spent the session discussing the difficulties in promoting social justice in the banking industry and had urged the participants to consider their own daily lives as proper arenas for social justice? Suppose the seminar had dealt with how to communicate to parishioners that their entire work lives—on the job, with the family, in the neighborhood—were opportunities for advancing social justice? Instead of advocating the formation of another parish committee, the instructor might have proposed ways a parish could support the laity's ordinary work in the world. Such an approach might broaden the responsibility for social justice from a few specialists on a social action committee to all Christians.

Committees sometimes distract the laity by mistaking church activity for effective action in the world. Too often these committees assume that elevated consciences and correct intentions will yield a just social order. Ian McCrae has pointed out the fallacy of thinking of social justice as a matter of good intentions:

> In gatherings of church activists one hears with increasing frequency the comment, "Our task is to be faithful, not successful." If the statement is intended to mean that in the pursuit of bringing a social action project to a successful conclusion, one should not act in ways which could be labeled "unfaithful," then the comment belongs in the "of course" category.
>
> But if as seems often the case, the remark implies that the religious actor will perform according to some divine ethical standard caring not whether the goal of the activity is achieved, then such a statement is patent nonsense.[3]

One would think that with all the talk about justice by the church in preparation and reflection, with all the church agencies which subscribe to that talk, with the prevalent teaching of the pope and bishops on the matter, the church would be a more effective agent in the quest for social justice. Unfortunately, it often seems that the church does not care about effectiveness at all.

To explain the term *social justice* some Catholic moralists contrast it with commutative justice and distributive justice.

Commutative justice is exercised when an exchange between two parties is on an equal plane. If a salesperson charges a customer a fair price and the customer pays the bill, the obligation of commutative justice has been fulfilled. If an employer exploits workers by paying too small a wage, or if a union demands an exaggerated pay scale, commutative justice has been violated. Fair prices, debt payments, just wages all are regulated by commutative justice. Obviously, no one argues with this concept in theory.

Distributive justice recognizes that there are relative differences among people. Rather than a strict *quid pro quo*, distributive justice makes compensation for these inequalities. An exceptional child, for example, needs more of society's resources than a normal child. Distributive justice is the obligation of an authority, perhaps a parent or a president, to distribute benefits to people in proportion to their abilities and needs. Distributive justice is the primary responsibility of government. There will always be loud arguments about how much compensation or affirmative action is fair, but most Americans have accepted the concept of distributive justice in fact if not in theory.

Social justice is not as well understood or accepted as commutative and distributive justice. It is often defined as the opposite of charity or social service. The Campaign for Human Development, for example, by addressing the causes of social problems, distinguishes itself from Catholic Charities, which treats the individual victims of social ills. Perhaps this distinction was helpful at a time when the church in preparation and reflection was neglecting the teaching of social justice. Such a limited understanding of social justice, however, does not sufficiently empower the laity to sustain and improve the world. The challenge of social justice, rather, is how to structure daily life. It is concerned with institutions because they establish the rules and standards (written or unwritten, formal or informal, highly visible or taken for granted) that govern how people act in various facets of life. Institutions can make living correctly either easy or difficult, for they are a necessary part of the environment in which people operate. The virtue of social justice aims at creating new institutions or changing old institutions so that the practice of all other virtues will be possible.

Here is an example from neighborhood living:

> Garbage is a problem in every community. Only a few years ago, St. Paul, Minnesota had no mandatory garbage collection. Each resident was allowed to hire or not hire independent collectors. Some people were too poor and others too lazy to dispose of their garbage properly. It is one thing to exhort individual residents to package and dispose of their garbage. It is quite another thing to establish regular and diligent garbage collection across an entire city at a reasonable cost to each resident. When those responsible in St. Paul organized to pass sanitation laws and set up systems to monitor just enforcement of those laws, they performed the act of social justice.

Many romanticists, including many well-intentioned church people, are very weak on the importance of institutions. Social justice for them becomes equated with a prophetic stance aimed at a change of heart in individuals, rather than dealing with institutions, which is more ambiguous. In fact, social justice seeks not so much to change people's internal feelings as to control the external effects of those feelings.

People can be virtuous, but only if they don't have to wake up every morning and make every moral decision all over again. We all need social reminders: laws, schools, media, trade organizations, consumer groups. These social reminders of virtue are called institutions, and social justice is about the creation, operation and ongoing reform of institutions.

The virtue of social justice sees to it that the obligations of commutative justice and distributive justice do not have to be thought out by every individual in each new situation.

Perhaps the best explanation of the distinctive virtue of social justice was provided by William Ferree, a Marianist priest who wrote in the '40s and greatly influenced American Catholic social thought.

Ferree gave this example. A businessman called *The Catholic Hour*, an old radio program. "I am trying to be a Christian at work, but the tide is running against me. Business ethics has been reduced to 'everybody's doing it.' If I don't do some questionable things, my competitor will and I'll be out of business. I have a family to support, a home to maintain, food and clothing to buy."

The answer given on the radio program was: "Right is right, even if nobody else does it. Wrong is wrong, even if everybody does it."

Ferree labeled this a "stupid" answer. The caller already knew right from wrong. What he was looking for was pastoral direction. Ferree mentioned three other inadequate responses that are still given to Christians in this everyday situation:

1. Do the best you can.

2. Go ahead and behave like everyone else. Under the principle of "double effect" it is not your primary intention to perpetuate the evil.

3. Quit your job.

The man's only real hope, Ferree maintained, was to take the situation out of the field of individual ethics. The businessman had to first understand the virtue of social justice and then exercise some calculated Christian courage.

On the basis of business ethics, the man was helpless in insuring justice and counteracting evil. If he were able, however, to organize a group of his fellow businesspeople, either in his own company or in several companies, and if the group was able to agree upon certain codes of conduct (no matter how minimal the restraint), that businessman would have begun to practice the virtue of social justice. In the very act of organizing he might have set in motion an institution that could insure justice for many years and many people.[4]

Social justice is not an optional call to some higher, extraordinary individual morality but a demand to do all that is necessary for the common good. While social justice is related to commutative justice, distributive justice, individual charity and social charity, it has a unique element, which is organization. When like-minded people interested in a virtue-supporting environment organize to create new institutions or reform existing ones, they practice social justice.

John Caron is president of a textile firm. He approaches the problem of plant closings from the point of view of a Christian manager. Although he genuinely tries to weigh the moral implications for himself and his business, it seems that he has to face his predicament alone: "A company cannot compete if the competitor's costs are inherently lower."[5]

If Caron could meet with managers of other companies, however, they might be able to practice social justice. If the group gathered by Caron, small as it might be, could agree on some mutual standards for layoff and closing notification, due compensation, reasonable rates of profit, and so forth, it would have made a major advance in the practice of social justice. The managers would remain competitors and must avoid the temptation of price-fixing and collusion, but they could institute some fair procedures for their competition which would give proper consideration to the larger community of humankind. The association of fair-minded textile plant owners that they instituted would be the fruit of their virtue.

One phenomenon of the inflation era has been the growth of community colleges. One such college had a student population of 2,000 in 1975 and 16,000 in 1985. With the increase of students came new faculty, many part time. In 1975 every teacher knew every secretary by name; in 1985 this was impossible. In 1975 secretaries were able to mimeograph and type on the spot; in 1985 this could no longer be done. Sometimes the expectations of the teachers, especially those who remembered the old days, were unrealistic. They demanded instant typing or duplication and expected the secretaries to pick up their payroll checks or provide other conveniences.

A group of secretaries got together and formed an informal association. They wrote a humorous job description for themselves. Although the list of "we do" and "we don't" was funny, its intention was serious and its effect important. That list, created in an organizational act of social justice, is now taped to every secretary's desk. The faculty is aware of the limits. The college has become more friendly and efficient; secretaries, professors, administration and students are more content.

Supervisors at a hospital were telling nurses to walk slowly when responding to a code on a certain floor. All the patients were elderly and their conditions were terminal. The supervisors knew that extreme life-saving measures were only prolonging the suffering of the patients and their families.

Some of the nurses were disturbed by this informal directive. They did not want a patient's death to be their responsibility. The situation became complicated when some nurses walked slowly while others ran. Guilt and second-guessing abounded.

Finally, some of the nurses organized a meeting at a nearby pizza parlor. The discussion continued long into the evening. Some of the exchanges were loud; some tears were shed. The consensus was that there was no consensus. The medical issue was too complicated to yield a principle that would cover each situation. Something did happen at that meeting, however, which exemplifies the key to social justice. The nurses decided that their collective behavior should be consistent. It would be important for all nurses at all times to respond to a code on that particular floor in the same way. Difficult situations were not eliminated, but subjective accusations, feelings of guilt and poor communications among nurses and with supervisors were minimized. Further, the nurses decided to reconvene their group at regular intervals to evaluate their decisions.

The standard procedure adopted at that informal meeting was the outcome of the practice of social justice. Those nurses who organized the pizza parlor meeting discovered the unique act of social justice—organization. By organizing, nurses would no longer harbor unreasonable guilt feelings nor could individuals be singled out as uncooperative by their supervisors. The discussion was now on the formal, public, institutional level where it belonged.

This does not mean that the work environment at that hospital is now unfriendly. By taking differences of opinion out of the realm of personalities, hospital relationships are now based on mutual respect and the common good. Social justice does not deny or eliminate disagreements or differences, however. The intent of social justice is not to make collective bargaining a merry affair. It is to encourage all parties to operate in the public arena, to recognize the legitimate interests of other sides in a dispute, and to disagree in a predictable, institutional manner.

It is incorrect to maintain, as do some conservatives, that owners have the moral right to make all decisions for a company provided they act in an ethical manner. It is equally wrong to hold, as do some liberals, that labor has a monopoly on truth provided it is reasonable in its demands. The virtue of social justice, in this case, allows the two parties—labor and management—to organize themselves in order to engage in collective bargaining. Social justice might also involve the organization of arbitration panels, regulatory agencies, or consumer pressure groups. Thus, social justice could be practiced by the participants on either or both sides, by outside mediators, by the government, by churches or other volunteer organizations interested in labor relations, by other companies or unions, by the media, or by any group acting to promote the common good.

These examples have involved practitioners of social justice working inside their normal occupational or life positions. This is not the only way to make a system more humane. At times it is absolutely necessary to goad a system from the outside in a prophetic, sometimes radical protest. Such extraordinary effort, however, should not be the normal method of operation in a good society. And even if outside protest is appropriate, it still takes people within the institutions to make the necessary correctives. For every Martin Luther King, Jr. there must be a Lyndon Baines Johnson.

It is necessary to highlight the role of the insider in achieving social justice because so much of the language and practice of the church in preparation and reflection suggests that protest and prophetic witness are the only vehicles for social justice. This was what the signers of the seminal *Chicago Declaration of Christian Concern* were complaining about:

> We also note with concern the steady depreciation, during the past decade, of the ordinary social roles through which the laity serve and act upon the world. The impression is often created that one can work for justice and peace only by stepping outside of these ordinary roles as a businessman, as a mayor, as a factory worker, as a professional in the State Department, or as an active union member and thus that one can change the system only as an "outsider" to the society and the system.
>
> Such ideas clearly depart from the mainstream of Catholic social thought which regards the advance of social justice as essentially the service performed within one's professional and occupational milieu. The almost exclusive preoccupation with the role of

the outsider as the model of social action can only distract the laity from the apostolic potential that lies at the core of their professional and occupational lives.[6]

The insider is the one who organizes institutions to be responsive to people. While there is a role for the prophetic outsider, most laypeople will be more effective, and therefore more virtuous, by practicing social justice in the ordinary institutions of their lives: job, family and neighborhood.

Yet the church in preparation and reflection is not adequately supporting a confident laity in the quest for social justice. Ed Marciniak charged that the disposition toward social change from the outside and against change from the inside may be deliberate:

> Among many church leaders and their staffs there lingers an abiding disdain for those Christians who work inside the political and economic system and a predilection for those who are stationed outside or against the system. Many of the church's civil servants (priests, religious and laity who are full-timers in the parish, diocesan office or the church-related hospital or school) operate with a built in bias. From the periphery of economic and political institutions they tend to stand in judgment and condemnation, not knowing how to commend, encourage or support the insiders, those businessmen, professional women and men, union leaders, who are persons of integrity and allergic to injustice.[7]

New York's John Cardinal O'Connor's treatment of New York Governor Mario Cuomo during the 1984 presidential election campaign was an example of this attitude. We must assume that O'Connor and Cuomo are equally sincere in their Christian faith and in their opposition to abortion. O'Connor, however, acting as the quintessential outsider on the issue, condemned all politicians who did not agree with his means of opposing abortion. A confident layman himself, Cuomo lashed out at "this whole notion that we are somehow 'failed Catholics' because we disagree with the bishops' political judgment. It's not good logic, it's not theologically sound, and it's not true."[8]

What should the church in preparation and reflection be doing to help the church at work in the world strive for social justice?

Education in the principles of justice would be paramount. It is, after all, in the busy world of everyday life that conflicting claims are bartered and systems for delivering human rights and needs are structured. In fact, considering all the socio-ethical decisions that Christians make every day in the medical labs, munition factories, research offices, health clinics, council chambers, classrooms, police beats, hospital wards and service agencies, parish social action committees can almost be a distraction. Training in the principles of justice might help Christians understand the ramifications of their daily work.

Social justice is not a weekend committee passing meaningless resolutions. Social justice is more than being aware of the events of the day. It requires moral courage, tact, ingenuity and a knowledge of attainable ends and workable tactics.

There are three basic elements to the successful practice of social justice.

1. *Organized Effort.* The virtue of social justice can be practiced either by forming new groups or by reforming existing groups. Social justice does not happen until people come together to tackle a mutual concern. A single person cannot be heard among the various interests in society: international markets, huge labor unions, giant corporations. It is necessary to get organized to have any voice and to make any contribution to the welfare of humankind. A just social order is not an extension of individual benevolence or individual justice.

2. *Institutional Reform.* It is not enough to fortify each individual. Too often the institutions of workplace, neighborhood and family take on lives of their own with patterns, rules and standards that are unexamined and unquestioned. To suggest, for example, that individuals monitor the content and duration of their television viewing misses the institutional nature of the television culture. There is a strong temptation to blame the individual victim in a situation, when in fact the institutions themselves must be challenged.

3. *Common Good.* The common good is more than the sum of each individual's good. The common good, the end of social justice, is the obligation both individuals and institutions have to structure society in such a way that commutative and

distributive justice can be practiced as easily as possible. Social conduct has to be regulated according to some code that fosters the good of all persons in society. While it is good for workers to make good salaries and manufacturers to make record profits, for example, if the needs of consumers in an inflationary market are not considered, the common good will fail. The common good, properly understood, brings about the greatest realization of particular goods, because in the real world the common good is ultimately based on the self-interests of all individuals. As St. Thomas Aquinas said, "Anyone who seeks the common good of a community thereby seeks his own good."[9]

Especially by using Catholic social teaching, the church in preparation and reflection can help the church at work in the world pursue the virtue of social justice. What is needed is not an attempt to make social justice one more church-run lay ministry program but rather specific programs to teach the value and skills of organization, the importance of institutions, and an appreciation of the common good. Social justice will then become the essence of the daily work of all confident laypeople.

Questions For Discussion

1) What did the term "social justice" mean to you? In what way has that understanding changed after reading this chapter?

2) Think of an example of a corporation or a social group that acknowledges social responsibility through a program that promotes social justice. Why does it support this program? Has the program been effective? If so, why?

3) Reflect on a way in which you can practically and effectively be involved in social justice in your daily life. How effectively can you work within your group or institution? Is there a point at which you believe that a reform effort from outside would be justified?

Chapter VI:
Social Teaching

Listen! I am sending you out just like sheep to a pack of wolves. You must be as cautious as snakes and as gentle as doves.

—*Matthew 10:16*

Over the centuries, but especially since the dawn of the industrial age, the daily efforts of the church at work in the world have yielded sound social principles, called Catholic social teaching or Catholic social thought. These principles are not dogmatic truths; they mean nothing unless they are adapted to new circumstances. With creative reapplication, however, Catholic social thought may provide a way out of the 20th century U.S. paradox of poverty amidst plenty.

There are several competing value systems in the United States, but the ascendent one is materialism. The forces of material success have been organized into mega-institutions such as multi-national corporations, the social service and medical industries, government and mass media. Individual laypeople often find themselves unable to negotiate with these often alienating structures, much less transform these institutions "in the manner of leaven." Many sincere people feel helpless against modern society because, trying to manage things alone, they are indeed powerless. Charles and Mary Ellen Wilber wrote:

> Christian responsibility or stewardship falls on infertile soil. . . . Since there are few avenues for exercising personal responsibility, the conscientious individual ends up feeling guilty. And unrelieved guilt leads to apathy and cynicism, which reinforces the dichotomization of life and further undermines Christian responsibility.[1]

A distinctive Catholic approach to addressing this form of powerlessness has been articulated as part of the church's social teaching. It is found in a group of phrases whose vitality seems to have been lost: the common good, personalism, pluralism, solidarity, solidarism, the organic society. Catholic social thought can best be understood not by contrasting these phrases, but by seeing them as a whole.

A central theme of Catholic social theory is encapsulated in the principle of subsidiarity given its classic formulation by Pope Pius XI:

> It is indeed true, as history clearly shows, that owing to the change in social conditions, much that was formerly done by small bodies can nowadays be accomplished only by large organizations. Nevertheless . . . it is an injustice and a grave evil and a disturbance of right order, to transfer to the larger and higher

collectivity functions which can be performed and provided for by lesser and subordinate bodies. Inasmuch as every social activity should, by its very nature, prove a help to members of the body social, it should never destroy or absorb them.[2]

While Pope Pius's phrasing today sounds archaic, it was a comprehensive statement of the experience of generations of the church at work in the world.

In their pastoral letter, "Economic Justice for All," the American bishops try to update the concept in these words: "In the principle of subsidiarity, Catholic social teaching has long stressed the importance of small- and intermediate-sized communities or institutions for the exercise of moral responsibility. These mediating structures link the individual to society as a whole in a way that gives people greater freedom and power to act."[3]

The genius of subsidiarity is that it recognizes that self-interest and social responsibility are not necessarily opposed to one another. Rejecting both collectivism and individualism, it finds in the nature of humankind an integrating principle that challenges people to be responsible, effective and friendly neighbors with one another. At the same time, "the principle of subsidiarity guarantees institutional pluralism, providing space for freedom, initiative and creativity."[4]

The debate in the United States over social policy has boiled down to a shouting match between liberals and conservatives over budgetary allocations, with the church in preparation and reflection often accepting the role of hospital for society's victims. To break the impasse between conservative individualism and liberal statism many are now searching for a third way, and finding answers in the Catholic social teaching of subsidiarity, which provides the philosophical underpinning for mediating structures. Mediating structures are institutions such as extended family, neighborhood, church and volunteer associations, which stand between the individual and the larger institutions of society. Unlike bureaucracies, mediating structures help people without impeding personal freedom. Mediating structures empower the average person trying to live in accord with Christian values.

The Chicago Project is an example of how the mediating structures approach can be used to empower the family. The Project, administered by Catholic Charities and funded by the U.S. Catholic Conference, the State Department's Bureau of Refugee Affairs, the Illinois Department of Public Aid and the Chicago Office of Refugee Resettlement, attempts to resettle Vietnamese, Laotian, Syrian and Rumanian refugees in such a way that they can avoid long-term dependency on public aid.

What the Chicago Project can do is train immigrants in marketable job skills before they become dependent on Refugee Cash Assistance, Medicaid, food stamps and AFDC. Sixty percent of all refugee families depend on public assistance for their entire first three years in America, yet the Chicago Project placed 75 percent of its refugees in jobs during its first three months. This feat was accomplished by controlling the purse strings. The Project dispensed all governmental money and benefits, but only if the refugee attended Project classes and fulfilled job-search requirements. The Project was able to keep close tabs on the refugee families through its church contacts in nearby neighborhoods.

The Brooklyn Ecumenical Cooperative is an example of a mediating structure which is renewing an urban neighborhood. The Cooperative has been able to broker the city government, the New York City Partnership (a business-backed civic organization), the New York State AFL-CIO and area banks to rehabilitate city-owned apartments for low- and moderate-income families. Each city-owned apartment is rehabilitated using a mixture of public and private funds and resold to families earning between $12,000 and $30,000 annually. Deposits in local banks by churches and unions encourage investment in the project. Unlike most government housing programs, the Cooperative's plan follows the principle of subsidiarity by keeping all power, decisions and responsibility at the lowest possible level.

The Naugatuck Valley Project, a coalition of church, labor, business and community groups in Connecticut, is an example of a mediating structure being used to empower industrial workers to deal with job creation and plant closings. By organizing a broad base of community support, including leveraging local governments for tax incentives, the Project was able to pull off one of the few successful workers' buyouts in the United States. Because of the mediation by the Project, the employees of Seymour Specialty Glass, formerly the Bridgeport Brass Company, were able to negotiate with the National Distillers Corporation to buy their own company and save 250 jobs in their community.

The principle of subsidiarity also holds the key to humanizing the large institutions of society. These megastructures, such as the international corporation, the modern military, the government bureaucracy, prize efficiency and routine. They often discourage innovation for fear that any changes might effect unforeseen consequences at another level of the organization. Morale within the megastructure and confidence about it in the wider society suffers when individual contributions and criticisms are neither expected nor appreciated. Subsidiarity could teach such institutions to organize so as to keep decision making at the lowest possible level.

Subsidiarity is not simply an argument for private ventures rather than public assistance. The ideological debate between liberals and conservatives misses the fact that private providers of services can be as impersonal as any government bureaucracy. Organized in one way, for example, neighborhood health clinics may be part of a mediating structures approach to neighborhood and family empowerment. Organized differently, these clinics could be just another way for some in the medical profession to enrich themselves at the expense of their patients and society. Adherence to the principle of subsidiarity will insure the former over the latter. A mediating structure must be organically related to the lives of the people it is serving. Every attempt at subsidiarity must seek the greatest participation in decision making by those who will be affected by the decisions.

Nor is the mediating structures approach simply an attempt to keep government out of the human service field.

> The principle of subsidiarity does not, however, support the view that the government which governs least governs best. . . .The challenge of today is to move beyond abstract disputes about whether more or less government intervention is needed to consideration of creative ways of enabling government and private groups to work together effectively.[5]

A confident, competent laity must support a social system which allows people to realize their own interest while at the same time seeking the common good. The Catholic social teaching of subsidiarity can provide the tools to accomplish that lofty goal. To bring about such a just society is the challenge for the lay church.

Questions For Discussion

1) What is your awareness of and familiarity with the church's social teachings?

2) How does a document like the Bishops' pastoral letter on the U.S. economy affect the church at work in the world? What is its effect on the rest of society?

3) What is your experience of the concept of subsidiarity or mediating structures in your daily life? How is this a Christian method of operation?

Conclusion:

A Sermon We'd Like to Hear

So God created human beings, making them to be like himself. He created them male and female, blessed them and said, "Have many children, so that your descendants will live all over the earth and bring it under their control."

—Genesis 1:27-28

"Whoever refuses to work is not allowed to eat." We say this because we hear that there are some people among you who live lazy lives and who do nothing except meddle in other people's business. In the name of the Lord Jesus Christ we command these people and warn them to lead orderly lives and work to earn their own living. But, you, sisters and brothers, must not become tired of doing good.

—2 Thessalonians 3:10-13

Jesus answered them, "My Father is always working, and I too must work."

—John 5:17

My sisters and brothers. One of our parishioners is a management advisor at a local company. The new municipal commercial tax which we voted to adopt in the recent election is affecting the company. To remain in our city, the company will have to raise its prices. Some managers of the company argue that they should abandon the city and move to where the tax rate is lower.

Our fellow parishioner is thinking about several good things:

—It is good for corporations to pay their fair share of taxes, so that the burden of municipal services will not fall entirely on the residents.

—It is good for corporations to remain in our city so that residents will have jobs.

—It is good for his company to provide quality goods and services at low prices for consumers.

—It is good for his company to make a fair profit.

Another parishioner is a mother of two sons and a daughter. The youngest son is in eighth grade. Her husband has moved out of the house. He has not been able to admit to himself that he is the victim of a disease—alcoholism. This woman is getting a lot of advice: divorce the bum; go back and finish college; plead with your husband for the sake of the children.

Our fellow parishioner is considering several good things:

—The promise she made to love her husband in sickness and in health.

—The good of her children.

—Her own emotional growth.

—Her husband's physical and spiritual health.

A third parishioner is very involved in a local community organization. Three weeks ago, his elderly mother—who is white—was mugged by two young men—who were black—across the street from our church building. He is torn by several impulses: Sell the family home and move out of this neighborhood; quit working with an organization which is perceived by some as racist; work harder within the organization to form coalitions between blacks and whites. He, too, is concerned about several good things:

—The safety and security of his family.

—The value of an integrated society.

—The equity in his home.

—The need for housing among many black families.

Each of our readings today tells us that these parishioners are God's church at work in the world.

In the reading from *Genesis*, we hear God's initial command to humankind: Fill the earth and subdue it. Use your God-given talent to bring the earth under your dominion. Make a home out of the earth. This making-over, this return to Eden, must be accomplished through human toil, through the sweat of our collective brow. It is in the very messiness of our daily work—on the job, with our families, in our neighborhoods—that we help bring about the kingdom of God "on earth, as it is in heaven."

Some people interpret the second reading as saying that Paul was against welfare: "Those who do not work, shall not eat." Paul was not commenting on welfare, for certainly he was a leader in collecting alms for the poor. He was lashing out against laziness. Some early Christians thought that Christ's Second Coming was so imminent that there was no need to work. Sit around and pray, they thought, until the end of the world. Paul reminded these Thessalonians of the God-given mandate to make the kingdom come through our work.

Jesus leaves no doubt about his meaning in our gospel: "My Father is still working and so am I." We are the Body of Christ. His creation begins each morning when you punch in at the job, when you get the kids off to school, when you check on a sick neighbor, when you work to make your community a little bit closer to that promised kingdom, which *Revelation* promises will begin here on earth.

All three of our parishioners—the business executive, the mother, the community activist—are trying to do God's will through their work. I can assure you that each of them is trying to shed the light of the Christian story on their individual predicaments. I can also assure you that each of them needs our help and prayers because they feel too much alone. As a parish, we must continue to support these three parishioners as they carry out the work of our church in the world.

The purpose of our congregation—the reason we exist and the reason we come together here to celebrate Mass—is to support the church, the people of God, at work in the world. We have photographs on our bulletin boards of many of you doing your daily work on your job, with your family and in our neighborhood. We designate different Sundays to honor different occupations: homemaker, social worker, parent, nurse, teacher, politician, laborer, manager, and others. We sponsor adult leadership training classes, community organizing efforts and support groups for various occupations and family groupings.

And this is why we celebrate the Eucharist together this morning. For the Eucharist means that our daily work can be sacramentalized. We consecrate into the body and blood of Christ the imperfect result of our work. We do not offer grapes and grain, we offer wine and bread. It takes human work to change grapes and grain into wine and bread. This is the mystery of the Incarnation: God comes and brings salvation, but only through human work, human labor. There was the labor of Mary, the labor of Joseph, the labor of Peter and the other fishermen, the labor of the tax collector Matthew, the tentmaker Paul, the doctor Luke, the labor of Martha and Mary, the labor of each of us. This is why we pray over the bread and wine: "We have this bread to offer which human hands have made. . . . We have this wine to offer, fruit of the vine, work of human hands."

As a parish we cannot solve the dilemmas of our three parishioners. Their solutions must be theirs as competent, confident laypeople. I know they will not find easy answers. I hope they won't get cheap advice. They will realize that their problems are not isolated and that institutions in our society will have to change if their individual problems are to be solved once and for all. They may need our congregation to help them mediate solutions.

We *can* do one thing for them. We can celebrate the fact that they are living full and complete Christian lives. I hope these three and all our parishioners find empathy and support from the church this week, the support and the wisdom of our Catholic tradition and community. Then it will mean something to them when we pray: "Go, the Mass is ended. God's work continues in our work."

Endnotes

Introduction

1. Vatican II, *Dogmatic Constitution on the Church*, No. 31.

2. National Catholic News Service, "Lay People Shouldn't Become Mini-Priests, Says a Bishop," *The Catholic Messenger*, January 10, 1985, p. 10.

Chapter I: Church

1. Vatican II, *Pastoral Constitution on the Church in the Modern World*, No. 43.

2. Ibid. No. 34.

3. Ibid. No. 39.

4. Maureen Dowd, "Cuomo in Pulpit, Talks of Ethics and Religion," *New York Times*, November 11, 1983, pp. 1 and 6.

5. Vatican II, *Decree on the Apostolate of the Laity*, No. 5.

6. Richard J. Mouw, *Called to Holy Worldliness* (Philadelphia: Fortress Press, 1980), p. 15.

7. John Coleman, *An American Strategic Theology* (Ramsey, NJ: Paulist Press, 1982), p. 53.

Chapter II: Vocation

1. Vatican II, *Dogmatic Constitution on the Church*, No. 10.

2. Russell Barta, "Developing Lay Leadership," in *The Catholic Laity Today: New Roles in the Church, New Challenges in Society* (Washington: FADICA, 1982).

3. Ed Marciniak, "On the Condition of the Laity," in Russell Barta (ed.), *Challenge to the Laity* (Huntington: Our Sunday Visitor Press, 1980), p. 35.

4. James Hoffman, "Called and Gifted: Empowerment of the Laity," Brooklyn, New York, 1983, p. 5.

5. Jean Haldane, "Faith, Learning and Ministry: Interrelated and Interdependent," *Origins*, February 21, 1985, p. 600.

6. Gary Bauler, "Official: Church Vocations Awareness Week," *The Tidings*, October 11, 1985, p. 5.

7. Mark Gibbs, *Christians With Secular Power* (Philadelphia: Fortress Press, 1981), p. 40.

Chapter III: Spirituality of Work

1. Pope John Paul II, *Laborem Exercens: On Human Work* (Boston: Daughters of St. Paul, 1981), pp. 63-64.

2. Vatican II, *Pastoral Constitution on the Church in the Modern World*, No. 34.

3. Pope John Paul II, *Laborem Exercens*, op. cit. p. 11.

4. Ibid. p. 56.

5. Martin Luther King, Jr., in Barbara Rowes (ed.), *The Book of Quotes* (New York: E.P. Dutton, 1979), p. 264.

6. Pope John Paul II, "The Gospel of Work," *Origins*, November 18, 1982, p. 374.

7. Teilhard de Chardin, *The Divine Milieu* (New York: Harper Torchbooks, 1960), p. 65.

8. The Labor Guild, "The Cushing-Gavin Award Brochure" (Boston: The Labor Guild, 1985).

Chapter IV: Self-Interest

1. Vatican II, *Pastoral Constitution on the Church in the Modern World*, No. 34.

2. Reinhold Niebuhr, in D.B. Robertson (ed.), *Love and Justice: Selections From the Shorter Writings of Reinhold Niebuhr* (Cleveland: The World Publishing Co., 1957), p. 27.

3. Andrew Greeley, *Building Coalitions: American Politics in the 1970s* (New York: New Viewpoints, 1974), pp. 136-137.

4. Michael Novak, *The Spirit of Democratic Capitalism* (New York: Simon and Schuster, 1982), p. 93.

5. Miriam Pawel, "Cuomo Dispenses Ecumenical Advice," *Newsday*, May 20, 1985, p. 17.

Chapter V: Social Justice

1. Vatican II, *Pastoral Constitution on the Church in the Modern World*, No. 30.

2. George Orwell, quoted in *Pocket Pal 1985* (Maywood: Myron Manufacturing Corp., 1984).

3. Ian J. McCrae, "Faithful or Successful?" *Coalition Close-Up*, Winter, 1984, p. 3.

4. William Ferree, S.M., *The Act of Social Justice* (Washington: Catholic University of America Press, 1942), pp. 69-71.

5. John B. Caron, "Noncompetitiveness Road to Oblivion," *National Catholic Reporter*, August 26, 1983, p. 17.

6. "The Chicago Declaration of Christian Concern," in Barta (ed.), op. cit. p. 23.

7. Ed Marciniak, "Being a Christian in the World of Work," *Origins*, July 19, 1982, p. 137.

8. Joan Barthel, "The Education of a Public Man," *Notre Dame Magazine*, Winter, 1984-85, p. 13.

9. Thomas Aquinas, *Summa Theologica*, (New York: Benzinger Brothers, Inc., 1947), p. 1395.

Chapter VI: Social Teaching

1. Charles and Mary Ellen Wilber, "The Economy, the Family, and Social Justice," in Stanley Saxton, et al. (eds.) *The Changing Family: Reflections on Familiaris Consortio* (Chicago: Loyola University Press, 1984), p. 67.

2. Pope Pius XI, *Quadragesimo Anno*, in William Gibbons, S.J. (ed.) *Seven Great Encyclicals* (Glen Rock, NJ: Paulist Press, 1963), p. 147.

3. United States Catholic Bishops, "Catholic Social Teaching and the U.S. Economy (Second Draft)," *Origins*, October 10, 1985, pp. 285-286.

4. Ibid. p. 270.

5. Ibid. p. 270.

Selected Bibliography

Prior to Vatican II, aside from some Catholic Action tracts, there were few resources specifically dealing with the role of the laity in and to the world. Even today, some 25 years later, there are only a handful of publications that address the practical implications of this lay vocation. Although a few are out of print, we have included here those resources helpful to us in thinking about the laity's mission to the world.

Books

Barta, Russell (ed.) *Challenge to the Laity*. Huntington, Indiana: Our Sunday Visitor Press, 1980.

Baum, Gregory. *The Priority of Labor*. Ramsey, New Jersey: Paulist Press, 1982.

Coleman, John. *An American Strategic Theology*. Ramsey, New Jersey: Paulist Press, 1982.

Congar, Yves. *Lay People in the Church*. Kansas City, Missouri: Leaven Press, 1985.

Curran, Charles. *American Catholic Social Ethics.* Notre Dame, Indiana: University of Notre Dame Press, 1982.

Diehl, William. *Christianity and Real Life.* Philadelphia, Pennsylvania: Fortress Press, 1976.

Diehl, William. *Thank God, It's Monday.* Philadelphia, Pennsylvania: Fortress Press, 1982.

Doohan, Leonard. *The Lay Centered Church.* Minneapolis, Minnesota: Winston Press, 1984.

Geaney, Dennis. *The Prophetic Parish.* Minneapolis, Minnesota: Winston Press, 1983.

Gibbs, Mark. *Christians With Secular Power.* Philadelphia, Pennsylvania: Fortress Press, 1981.

Greeley, Andrew. *The Communal Catholic.* New York, New York: Seabury Press, 1976.

Greeley, Andrew. *The American Catholic.* New York, New York: Basic Books, 1977.

Greeley, Andrew. *American Catholics Since the Council.* Chicago, Illinois: Thomas More Press, 1985.

Heiges, Donald. *The Christian's Calling.* Philadelphia, Pennsylvania: Fortress Press, 1984.

Heisler, W.J. and John Houck (eds.). *A Matter of Dignity*. Notre Dame, Indiana: University of Notre Dame Press, 1977.

Hollenback, David. *Claims in Conflict*. Ramsey, New Jersey: Paulist Press, 1979.

Houck, John and Oliver Williams. *Co-Creation and Capitalism: John Paul II's "Laborem Exercens."* Lanham, Maryland: University Press of America, 1983.

Kinast, Robert. *Caring for Society*. Chicago, Illinois: The Thomas More Press, 1985.

Marciniak, Ed. *Tomorrow's Christian*. Dayton, Ohio: Pflaum Press, 1969.

Maritain, Jacques. *Reflections on America*. New York, New York: Gordian Press, 1975.

Monsma, Stephen. *Pursuing Justice in a Sinful World*. Grand Rapids, Michigan: William Eerdmans Publishing Co., 1984.

Mouw, Richard. *Called to Holy Worldliness*. Philadelphia, Pennsylvania: Fortress Press, 1980.

Murray, John Courtney. *We Hold These Truths*. Kansas City, Missouri: Sheed and Ward, 1985.

Novak, Michael. *The Spirit of Democratic Capitalism*. New York, New York: Simon and Schuster, 1982.

Novak, Michael. *Freedom With Justice: Catholic Social Thought and Liberal Institutions*. New York, New York: Harper and Row, 1984.

O'Brien, David. *The Renewal of American Catholicism*. Ramsey, New Jersey: Paulist Press, 1972.

Peck, George and John Hoffman (eds.). *The Laity in Ministry*. Valley Forge, Pennsylvania: Judson Press, 1984.

Pierce, Gregory. *Activism That Makes Sense: Congregations and Community Organization*. Ramsey, New Jersey: Paulist Press, 1984.

Stevens, R. Paul. *Liberating the Laity: Equipping All the Saints for Ministry*. Downers Grove, Illinois: Intervarsity Press, 1985.

Varacalli, Joseph. *Toward the Establishment of Liberal Catholicism in America*. Lanham, Maryland: University Press of America, 1983.

Vos, Nelvin. *Seven Days a Week*. Philadelphia, Pennsylvania: Fortress Press, 1985.

Vos, Nelvin. *Monday's Ministries: The Ministry of the Laity*. Philadelphia, Pennsylvania: Parish Life Press, 1979.

Williams, Oliver and John Houck (eds.). *The Judeo-Christian Vision and the Modern Corporation*. Notre Dame, Indiana: University of Notre Dame Press, 1982.

Wills, Garry. *Bare Ruined Choirs*. New York, New York: Delta Publishing, 1971.

Woodward, Irene (ed.). *The Catholic Church: The United States Experience*. Ramsey, New Jersey: Paulist Press, 1979.

Articles

Barta, Russell. "Let Laypersons Minister in the Marketplace," *St. Anthony's Messenger*, March 1979.

Barta, Russell. "Work: In Search of New Meanings," *Chicago Studies*, August 1984.

Barta, Russell. "Liberation: USA Style," *America*, April 13, 1985.

Bernardin, Joseph. "Executives Must Practice Religious Beliefs at Work," *Crain's Chicago Business*, December 26, 1983.

Cuomo, Mario. "The Confessions of a Public Man," *Notre Dame Magazine*, Winter 1984-85.

Droel, William. "A Reappraisal of the Permanent Diaconate," *America*, January 28, 1984.

Droel, William. "Northern Liberation Theology," *America*, January 26, 1985.

Droel, William. "The Delivery of Human Service: Mediating Structures and Catholic Social Thought," *Communio*, Spring 1984.

Droel, William. "The Vocation Crisis," *Pastoral Life*, July/August 1983.

Droel, William. "Ministering to the Successful," *Pastoral Life*, September 1984.

Droel, William and Gregory Pierce. "Accountable Economics," *Catholicism and Crisis*, October 1983.

Droel, William and Gregory Pierce. "Tradition Should Not Be Given Short Shrift," *National Catholic Reporter*, November 18, 1983.

Droel, William and Gregory Pierce. "The Great Workbench," *America*, August 4-11, 1984.

Foley, Jerry. "Monday Morning Ministry," *Today's Parish*, October 1985.

Hebblethwaite, Margaret. "Towards a New Theology of the Laity," *The Tablet*, June 1, 8, 15, 1985.

Marciniak, Ed. "Being a Christian in the World of Work," *Origins*, July 29, 1982.

Marciniak, Ed. "Workin' 9 to 5: Is there a way to be a Christian?" *U.S. Catholic*, September 1984.

Pierce, Gregory. "A Spirituality of St. Joseph the Worker," *America*, June 2, 1984.

Speeches

Bernardin, Joseph. "The Future of Church and Ministry," *Origins*, March 26, 1982.

Hoffman, James. "Called and Gifted: Empowerment of the Laity," St. James Cathedral, Brooklyn, New York, April 24, 1983.

May, John. "Keynote Address to Archdiocesan Council on the Laity," St. Louis, Missouri, March 1981.

McDermott, John. "Weakness Amidst Strength: The Catholic Paradox," speech at Chicago Theological Union, May 27, 1983.

Starpoli, Frank. "Inverted Vision and the Response of the Institution," Rochester, New York, March 24, 1984.

Van Allen, Rodger. "The Chicago Declaration and the Call to Holy Worldliness," speech to College Theology Society, June 2, 1984.

Newsletters

Between Sundays. William Farley, 16 Saw Mill Road, West Simsbury, Connecticut 06092.

Centering. The Center for the Ministry of the Laity, 210 Herrick Road, Newton Centre, Massachusetts 02159.

Gifts. U.S. Bishops Committee on the Laity, 1312 Massachusetts Avenue NW, Washington, D.C. 20005.

Initiatives. National Center for the Laity, 14 E. Chestnut Street, Chicago, Illinois 60611.

Laity Exchange. Vesper Society, 311 MacArthur Boulevard, San Leandro, California 94577.

Monday's Ministers. Laos in Ministry, 231 Madison Avenue, New York, New York 10016.

Pamphlets

The Catholic Laity Today. Washington, D.C.: Foundations and Donors Interested in Catholic Activities (FADICA), 1982.

Chicago Declaration of Christian Concern. Chicago, Illinois: The National Center for the Laity, 1977.

The New American Catholic: The Challenge of Power and Responsibility, Chicago, Illinois: The National Center for the Laity, 1986.

Magazine Special Issues

"American Spirituality," *New Catholic World*, July/August 1982.

"The Laity," *New Catholic World*, May/June 1984.

Church Documents

John Paul II. *On Human Work*. New York, New York: Daughters of St. Paul Editions, 1981.

National Conference of Catholic Bishops of the United States. *Called and Gifted: The American Catholic Laity*. Washington, D.C.: U.S. Catholic Conference, 1980.

Vatican Synod Secretariat. *The Laity's Vocation and Mission: Synod 87 Lineamenta, Origins,* February 1985.

Vatican II. *Dogmatic Constitution on the Church; Pastoral Constitution on the Church in the Modern World; Decree on the Apostolate of the Laity.* In Walter Abbott, ed. *The Documents of Vatican II.* New York, New York: America Press, 1966.